# Lessons from Nature
# Dr. Fox's Fables

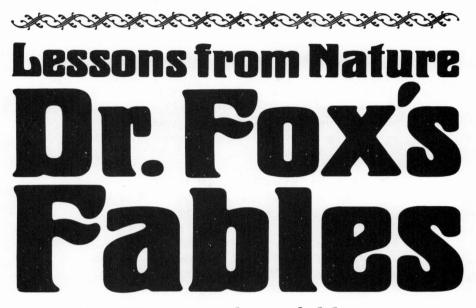

# Lessons from Nature
# Dr. Fox's Fables

*Twenty-three fables
in which animals talk about
how they really feel
and live.*

## Dr. Michael W. Fox

*Director,
Institute for the Study
of
Animal Problems*

**ACROPOLIS BOOKS LTD.** Washington, D.C. 20009

**ACROPOLIS BOOKS LTD.**
Colortone Building, 2400 17th St., N.W.
Washington, D.C. 20009

Printed in the United States of America by
**COLORTONE PRESS, Creative Graphics Inc.**
Washington, D.C. 20009

**Library of Congress Cataloging in Publication Data**

Fox, Michael W.          1937-
    Dr. Fox's fables.

    SUMMARY: Twenty-two fables explore relationships between animals and between animals and man.
    1.  Fables, American.  [1.  Fables]  I.  Title.
PZ8.2.F66   [Pic]   80-18345
ISBN 0-87491-291-1
ISBN 0-87491-516-3 (pbk.)

# TABLE
# OF
# CONTENTS

# Animals of Foreign Lands

# PREFACE

here are many definitions of "fable" in *Webster's International Dictionary,* one being, "a narration intended to enforce some useful truth or precept." Another more common perception of the fable is a story in which "animals and even inanimate objects speak and act like human beings," such as in Aesop's fables. In other words, they are anthropomorphic, the animals (or objects) being personified as humans or as having certain human qualities. Most fables about animals are,

therefore, highly anthropomorphic; and I believe that this can be extremely misleading to readers both young and old. Animals are not little people. When we distort their true nature by making them anthropomorphic, we limit the real learning and insights that might be gained by a more accurate knowledge of their ways and nature. Worse, children may well acquire a totally false, human-centered regard for animals.

My fables are primarily animal-centered, *zoomorphic* rather than *anthropomorphic:* my animals think and act as animals rather than as human beings. In these animal-centered fables, the animals speak for themselves as animals and not as little people, thus opening the door into their world for us to learn. These fables, which I regard as ''lessons from nature,'' can also open the door into our own consciousness and give us a deeper understanding of our own nature, for we too are animals.

Readers, in gaining a clear insight into the ways of animals, can discover something of themselves in the animal. The animal thus becomes a teacher, and a connection with nature is established. By learning about animals, their instincts and their behavior, we can glean many insights into our own nature and perhaps, more important still, acquire a deeper understanding and respect for our animal kin. It would seem that, considering the ways in which both wild and domestic animals are exploited and abused today, people have little reverence for life. These fables will, I hope, help foster such reverence through understanding the whys and ways of our animal kin.

Dr. Michael W. Fox
Director,
*Institute for the Study of Animal Problems*
Washington, D.C.

# ANIMALS
# ARE
# LIKE PEOPLE

# ANIMALS ARE PEOPLE TOO!

o you know how much animals are like people? Or, put another way, how much people are like animals? All animals communicate with each other in one way or another. Communicating means telling something about yourself, how you feel, what you want or what you intend to do. Like you and me, they howl or whine when they are lonely, cry when they are hurt and scream when they are afraid. They and we, also moan and wail for attention and make

all kinds of giggling and whooping sounds when happy or in a playful mood.

Just as you and me, animals don't like to be cold or hungry; they like to be comfortable, well-fed, and with their friends. Some live in big cities, like bees in their hives and termites in their castles. Others live together in big families, like the wolves and chimpanzees, where aunts and uncles take care of the youngsters and will often act as babysitters! In some societies, like baboon troops and wolf packs, there is a leader who often acts like a policeman and breaks up fights.

Young animals, like young people, like to play. Chimps and wolf cubs like to wrestle and play hide-and-seek; lambs play tag and "king of the castle;" baby badgers play roly-poly and leapfrog, and young otters love to play on mud slides.

*Lessons From Nature*

Although they may look the same to you (and I'm sure you and your friends do to them), underneath their uniform spots, or stripes, or browns, or grays, are many differences. Some animals, like some of your friends, tend to be more greedy, bossy, jealous or rough; while others are shy, or gentle, or curious, or more playful than others.

Yes, animals are not only like people, they are our brothers and have as much right as you and I to live peacefully in this world. In an old Indian tale a coyote spoke of men and animals. The coyote came to an Indian boy while he was asleep out on the plains and he said, "Know me, friend, I am your brother; let us share this world, there is no other!"

# THE SKUNK WHO WANTED TO BE DIFFERENT

"But mother," complained Stripey, a young skunk, "I don't want to look just like everybody else with these stupid ordinary white stripes on my sides. I want to be different."

"I'm sorry dear, but that's the way you were made. You are a striped skunk. You don't have teeth like a wolf, antlers like a stag, or claws like a bobcat to defend yourself with. Your only protection is your stink gun."

11

## The Skunk Who Wanted to be Different

Stripey's mother was referring to the scent gland under skunks' tails. Skunks can shoot the scent from the gland at enemies and drive them off with the horrible smell.

"I know all about that mother and that's just fine, but what about these stripes? They'll have to go," Stripey continued.

"No, dear. You see, your stripes warn enemies that you have a concealed weapon. When they see your stripes, they will keep away. If you didn't have your stripes, they might kill you with one bite before you could shoot them with stink."

Stripey trotted off, tail defiantly up in the air, thinking to himself, "I'm a skunk, stripe or no stripes and they have got to go."

He found a tall ant hill built of red earth and decided to rub his sides against it. His fur was still wet with morning dew from the grass, and the red earth stuck easily to his coat. Soon his coat was quite red and all traces of warning stripes had been covered.

Stripey proudly trotted back to his mother. At first she didn't recognize him and was afraid and ran to hide under a bush. He turned around in the open and said, "See mother, I'm different now." Before she could come to her senses and could scold him, a bobcat leaped into the clearing and grabbed Stripey by the tail. He let out a scream; and at once his mother ran out backwards, tail up, aiming her 'gun' with deadly accuracy into the eyes of the surprised cat. The bobcat dropped Stripey and ran off hissing and pawing madly at its face.

"See what I mean?" asked his mother sternly. "Now you run through the wet grass until all that stuff comes off. I don't want to see you again until your stripes are spotless.''

Stripey did as he was told. He never wanted to be without his stripes again.

# THE HARE
# AND
# THE TORTOISE

"owdy, slowcoach," mumbled a young hare through a mouthful of clover. He was addressing an old and wise tortoise who chose to ignore the hare. He leisurely continued to eat his dinner of clover buds.

"Jeepers, you even eat in slow motion. Say, I heard of some creepy tortoise who once ran a race with a hare and won. How about that for a phony fable!"

*Lessons From Nature*

The hare jumped over the tortoise and raced around several times before coming to a screeching halt right in front of him. "See, I'm fast. I'm the fastest thing around on four legs."

"Mmmm," sighed the tortoise as he bit into a sweet clover bud. He still ignored the hare who continued to show off and tease him.

"Glad you agree," said the hare. "Guess you must get pretty tired carrying that silly house around on your back all the time. Why not step out of it for a while, and we'll have a race. I'll give you a fair head start."

This remark about his "house" was the last straw for the tortoise. He looked at the hare with his solemn eyes and said with slow dignity, "Young man, your safety is your speed and mine is my shell; or, as you in your ignorance call it, my house.''

''You're just too cowardly to come out,'' teased the hare. ''Look at me, I'm fast and I'm free.''

Just then a coyote cub, who had been watching the hare and the tortoise for some time, leaped at them. The quick hare skipped easily out of the way, and the cub grabbed at the tortoise instead. With his head, tail and legs tucked inside his hard shell he was safe. The cub chewed and poked and rolled him all over the place trying to get him out, but without success.

The hare squatted close by and laughed. ''See old tortoise, the secret to success is speed.'' He sat back on his haunches and watched the cub and the tortoise with amusement. Hare was so involved watching that he didn't notice the cub's mother creeping up behind him. She grabbed the hare, and at once the cub forgot all about the tortoise. The two coyotes had hare for dinner, right then and there.

"What was that you said?" asked the tortoise, coming slowly out of his shell and looking around for the hare, "The secret to success is speed?" When there was no answer, he noticed the two coyotes eating.

"Yes," said the mother coyote. "But as you know, old tortoise, you have to use your wits as well, speed is not everything!"

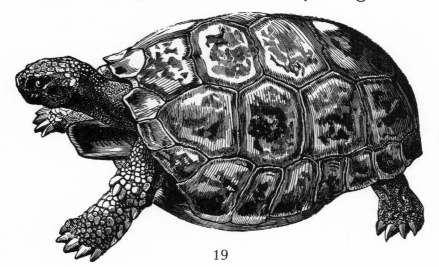

# THE SQUIRREL AND THE SPARROW

It was many weeks before winter, but on this bright crisp morning some of the animals in the forest knew that it would not be too long in coming. A sparkling carpet of frost covered the fallen leaves on the ground, and all the yellow stems of grass were shimmering like polished silver and gold. It was the first time for many of the younger animals to walk, hop, skip or crawl on the frozen earth.

A squirrel, who was born earlier that year, came cautiously down his tree and sniffed curiously. He reached out to touch the frosty mantle covering the brown leaves at the base of the tree trunk. He had never seen anything like this before in his whole long life of seven months. The icy frost on his nose made him sneeze; and as he sat up to rub it with his front paws, he felt the frost nipping his hind feet. He jumped high in the air in surprise, wondering what invisible creature had bitten him. His jump carried him into a thick clump of grass; and when he emerged he was covered in white frost.

A fat young sparrow, who had been watching his friend's antics, twittered in amusement, "Oh, you funny fellow, haven't you seen frost before?"

"No," retorted the squirrel, "and neither have you. The day after I came out of the nest, you hatched out of an egg in the same tree. So I'm a day older than you, and I haven't seen the likes of this before. That means you haven't either!''

''But I was laid in the nest before you ever came out into the world, so I am older and know more than you anyway,'' argued the sparrow. He always liked to start the day arguing with the first person he met, and that was usually Squirrel.

''Have it your way! There's no point in arguing with you since you always win. My feet are getting cold,'' and with a flick of his tail, Squirrel started rummaging around under the tree.

''What on earth are you doing now?'' inquired cheeky Sparrow, who always delighted in following Squirrel everywhere and prodding and teasing him with questions and riddles. "When is a sparrow not a sparrow?" he asked Squirrel.

"When it's an egg—I've heard that one before. Please leave me alone. I've got work to do," chattered Squirrel.

"What are you doing anyway? I've never seen you so busy," Sparrow exclaimed.

"I feel like collecting nuts and seeds; and I'm going to work all day and hide them around here in holes that I must dig. Please go away, I've got lots of work to do. And don't ask me why I'm doing it. I just have to. Something inside me tells me that I should."

"The frost has affected your mind young squirrel, you're crazy. There's plenty of food around. Live now and don't worry about tomorrow. It will take care of itself, that's my motto. Save for a rainy day and it will never rain. See you around, old worry-bag.'' With a raucous laugh Sparrow twittered off to find breakfast.

As winter came, the sun took longer to come up over the trees to warm the forest, and food became harder and harder to find. Animals need food to keep warm in the winter. Even thick fur or feather coats are not enough to keep away the penetrating cold. This particular winter, many animals had already gone to sleep. Others who had not hibernated had migrated to warmer regions in the south where food would be plentiful.

When the days were dark and cold, Squirrel would sleep, sometimes for days on end, warm and snug in a nest of leaves and twigs. His bushy tail, such a useful signal to express to others how he felt, now served as a blanket for his head and feet. His sleep was so deep, like that of a hibernating ground hog, he didn't need much food. But on sunny days he would wake briefly and have a snack from one of his well-hidden food stores. On one of these days he met Sparrow again.

"How quiet you are Sparrow. No riddles today?" he asked, as he nibbled an acorn. Sparrow gave a plaintive "cheep," and said that he was hungry. "But you look so fat," said Squirrel through a mouthful of delicious mushy acorn.

"It's just my feathers I fluff out to keep warm," sighed Sparrow.

"Well, don't just perch there sighing and fluffing. Come on over and tuck in."

"Thank you," said Sparrow, and he ate with the Squirrel until he was almost ready to burst.

That meal saved his life; without it Sparrow would have died from the cold that night. "I will never tease squirrels again for saving for the cold days," he chirruped. "You and your kind are indeed wise to do that. Perhaps we sparrows might learn one day. Thank you again, dear friend." He flew off knowing that he would see the spring soon because the buds on the tree where he and Squirrel lived were showing green at last.

# THE FOX
# AND
# THE OPOSSUM

uietly, deep within the forest a red fox was hunting for breakfast. Suddenly he saw a movement in the bushes. Stealthily, Foxy stalked to the bushes, trying as best he could to make no noise on the dry leaves that rustled with soft crackling sounds under his feet with each step.

When he reached the bushes, there was nothing to be seen, but his nose told him that somewhere nearby was a 'possum. He

29

sniffed around for a long time. Suddenly he stepped on something soft and warm and furry. Foxy jumped back in surprise. Possum lay half covered by leaves and seemed to be very dead. He didn't move even when Foxy jabbed him with a paw.

Foxy didn't want to eat anything that looked so dead but smelled so alive. He only liked to grab things that moved, because that way he knew they were fresh and tasted good.

Foxy didn't know that Possum was playing his usual trick of pretending to be dead. Opossums will do this when they are scared; and when Possum first saw Foxy, he was very scared. Immediately he curled up and played dead.

Foxy was very puzzled indeed, and he left Possum to find his breakfast somewhere else.

## Lessons From Nature

As soon as Foxy had left and all was quiet again, Possum uncurled himself, cautiously sniffed the air, and then raced up the nearest tree.

Sometime later Foxy passed by that tree on his way home. He was still hungry, having only caught a mouse and a couple of frogs for breakfast. His senses were still on the lookout for food. His keen eyes caught the 'possum's movements as it crawled along a branch.

Foxy stood under the tree. Looking up in amazement, he exclaimed, "I thought you were dead Possum, or was that your identical twin I found under the bushes?"

Possum squinted down at the fox, his beady eyes watering in the sunlight. He preferred to be out at night and in the sunshine he couldn't see as well as in darkness.

He opened his mouth and laughed at Foxy and in a slow and rusty voice said, ''Yes, my foxy foe, it was me and I tricked you by pretending to be dead!''

Suddenly, Foxy began to chase his tail. He leaped into the air, made a nose dive into the ground and rolled over. Then he chased his tail again. It was like a crazy dance. Perhaps foxes first started to do this when they were frustrated by not being able to reach something they wanted. But Foxy knew that this dance could lure an unwary duck or rabbit close enough for him to be able to seize it.

Possum became very curious and lost all sense of danger. What was there to fear when the fox had turned into a crazy clown?

Slowly he crawled down the branch to get close enough for a better view. Possum didn't notice that with each roll Foxy was edging a little closer to the tree. Suddenly Foxy shot like an arrow and grabbed the un-wary 'possum.

"How's that for a trick, Possum? I'm not called Foxy for nothing," he said, and promptly ate the 'possum.

# THE SEALS
# AND
# THE SEA OTTER

"Just look at that ugly fellow," barked the seal to his young cousin swimming nearby. He pointed a flipper at a long, furry animal lying on its back in the water.

"Hey, dog's body, what are you doing out here? It's deep and you might drown," the second seal shouted.

They were teasing a sea otter who was floating peacefully in the water on his back. He had a stone resting on his chest for no apparent reason.

*The Seals and The Sea Otter*

"I can swim quite well, thank you, and I don't think I will drown. I was born in the sea you know," replied the sea otter.

Then the first seal said, "Yes, my mother told me of you dogs' bodies who live around the kelp beds, but you're the first I've seen and you are weird."

"Look at us, we are built smooth and streamlined for super speed, so we can catch all the fish we want," boasted the second seal as he dived and twisted in the water. "Your head's too big, your hair's too long and you have hands, not flippers. Crawl back on land, buddy, and stay there. The ocean is no place for the likes of you!" he said.

"I can do just as well in the ocean as any of you, I assure you, dear seals," the old otter replied. "Although I may look very odd to you fellows, I don't have to look just like

36

you in order to live a happy and successful life in the sea. You're prejudiced.''

''Prejudiced?'' said the seals in one voice, ''What does that mean?''

''It means,'' said the old sea otter, ''that you don't like me because I don't look like you. Now it is true that seals once lived on the land, because like me, you are warm-blooded. But you seals have been living in the sea millions of years longer than us sea otters.''

''So that means we're better,'' said one seal. And the other barked, ''And we were here first, so the sea is ours.''

''Perhaps,'' replied the sea otter, ''But the whales and the dolphins have been living in the ocean even longer. It's for all of us to share. And you know,'' he said with a grin, ''the longer you live in the sea, the more you evolve to look like a fish. Look at your-selves—you boys haven't even any ears or fingers and toes!''

The sea otter laughed and dived. After a long, long while he surfaced with a large abalone shell. The young seals looked on in amazement as he rolled onto his back and proceeded to beat the abalone against the stone 'anvil' on his chest. This way he could break it open and eat the delicious meat in-side. The hungry seals looked on in surprise and envy as the otter feasted. They had never seen a sea otter before and had never seen any animal use a stone as a tool. What a wise and intelligent sea-dog he was!

When the sea otter dived again, the seals swam away together to hunt for their own dinner, with a new respect for the dog's body of the sea.

"I guess it doesn't matter how you look so long as you can do things well," said the first seal.

"Humph, I guess you're right," said the second. "Don't judge a fellow on first impressions, that's for sure! I really don't mind sharing the oceans with someone like that. It would be boring if we all looked alike, wouldn't it?"

# THE ROOK
# AND THE
# SONG THRUSH

he young rook was taking a luxurious bath in a dry puddle of mud. The powdery mud, just like talcum powder, removed grease and dirt from his feathers. He wriggled his chest and flapped his wings, rubbing the dust deep into his ruffled feathers. His eyes were half-closed in pleasure. After awhile he shook himself and preened his feathers thoroughly, using his beak like a comb to smooth out each feather. Soon he was looking very smart indeed; his

black, iridescent feathers glistened and flashed in the sunlight. He let out a loud "caaw"
of delight.

A thrush perched in a nearby persimmon
tree began to sing its early-morning song. It
sang long and melodiously and the rook
marveled at his skill.

"What a beautiful voice you have, Mr.
Thrush. You must have to practice a long
time to sing so well."

"But, of course," whistled the thrush.
"It takes a lot of practice to be good at
anything, but also, I have natural talent for
singing. I'm not called a Song Thrush for
nothing, you know," he added arrogantly.

"I see," cawed the rook. "Tell me, If I
practiced, could I sing like you?"

"Oh no, of course not," replied the
thrush. "You have no natural talent for

singing, of course. You and your cousins, the ravens and crows, are a very uneducated and untalented bunch of feathers. There's no hope for you, of course.'' Insulted, the raven ruffled his feathers but quickly regained his composure.

''Why do you sing, Mr. Thrush?'' the rook asked politely. ''Do you sing for fun?''

''For fun! Of course not. This is serious business. I sing to tell others that I am here, of course; and that this is *my* singing tree and *my* area where *I* live. Of course, I sing to keep rivals away and to attract a mate; and, of course, young lady thrushes love my voice and come flocking to me in the springtime.''

''That sounds like hard work to me, singing just to impress others. I mean, to have to be a perfectionist. Is it really worth it? Can't you just enjoy it?'' said the rook, carefully preening one wing feather that insisted on curling up the wrong way. ''I just caw for pleasure with my friends in the rookery where we all nest and ca-caw together, high in the elm trees in the evening. It's a happy occasion for all of us. I wish I could sing as prettily as you, but all this talk of work and social status seems to take the fun out of it.'' The rook flew off, his broad wings flashing in the sunlight. He rose into the sky cawing loudly to his friends in the elm trees.

''Noisy fool,'' thought the thrush, as he began to sing again, not knowing that rooks and crows are some of the most intelligent birds and that they live for many, many years.

## Lessons From Nature

''Don't judge a fellow by what he can or can't do,'' piped a cheeky little sparrow who had been watching the rook and the thrush all the time. ''The rook envied you until he found out why you sing.''

The thrush puffed out his speckled chest and exclaimed, ''Of course, of course not,'' and resumed his singing, knowing that if he didn't sing, he would soon lose his place to another thrush. Would he ever know what it would be like just to sing or caw for pleasure and ca-caw with friends like the rook?

''Only fools can't sing,'' he whistled.

''Of course, of course not,'' echoed the sparrow, but the thrush was lost in his song and heard nothing except himself and his own importance. Perhaps one day he would learn to sing for singing's sake just because it felt good and gave others pleasure.

# THE PORCUPINE AND THE DEER

On a misty autumn morning Porky, the porcupine, was on his way to take a drink at his usual place by the stream. Last night had been a long and scary night indeed. A young cougar or mountain lion, had discovered Porky grubbing around for food under a rock, and had cornered him there half the night. Porky, who was as fat as he was prickly, was frightened by the bold cougar's terrifying roars and hisses. But he was safe under the rock as long as he kept his back of quills turned out toward the big cat. When it swiped at him with one powerful paw and got a pad full of sharp quills, its screams filled the valley. The more it hurt, the more the cougar tried to reach in and pull poor Porky out of his refuge under the rock.

After what seemed like half a lifetime, the crazed cougar gave up and limped away, sniffling and growling. Porky hoped the mountain lion would return to its mountain retreat to nurse its wounds.

When he felt the coast was clear, Porky crawled cautiously out of hiding, but as he wobbled down to the stream he began to puff up with pride.

"Why," he thought, "I fought off a mountain lion today. I must be the bravest of all the animals in the valley." Lost in these high ideas about himself, he almost slipped down the muddy bank head first into the stream.

"Those deer," he muttered through his long, yellow front teeth. "They make such a muddy mess around this place."

"Oh, I'm so sorry, so sorry, but this is the only safe place for us to drink along the river," replied a little spotted deer from the shadows of a tall fir tree. "You see," she continued, "anywhere else a cougar can lie in ambush in the rocks and catch us as we drink."

"I don't care a quill," said the porcupine, wiping his muddy paws. "You and the rest of your skittish friends will have to move on. I have such short legs and my tummy gets so wet and muddy. You do just fine with those long legs of yours."

## The Porcupine and The Deer

Then Porky puffed himself up and told the deer how brave he had been fighting the mountain lion. "You deer just run away. You are such a timid bunch of cowards," he concluded.

"Our speed is our only defense. You have your armor of thorns," the deer replied.

"No, I am brave and you are all cowards because you always run away. And they are quills, not thorns. Do you think I'm a cactus?"

Porky drank noisily from the stream and then waddled arrogantly away, throwing a last quip at the deer. "Remember, I am the bravest of all and don't muddy up *my* drinking place again. Run away, coward, before I prick your legs."

The next morning the deer went to drink at the same place, for there was no other safe place to go. There she found the remains of Porky. The tracks in the mud showed that he had been killed by a coyote. Wise coyotes know how to flip a porcupine over and bite into its soft belly where there are no quills.

"Poor porcupine," said the deer to herself. "He saw my running away as being cowardly, but I will live. He thought no one could hurt him, since his armor kept the mountain lion away. How wrong he was! To be always afraid and run for your life is safer than to believe that a few thorns will keep all hunters away."

Just then a twig snapped nearby, and the deer ran for her life into the cover of the forest. It was only a squirrel, but it could have been the cougar stalking her. Better to be afraid and *live,* then foolishly brave and *die.*

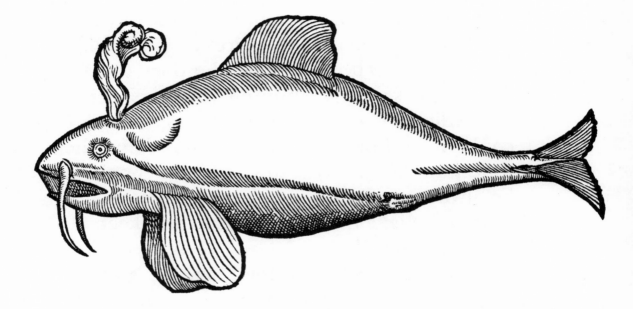

# THE WHALE
# AND
# THE SHRIMP

aking up the song as he went along, an enormous whale named Humpety (because he was a hump-backed whale) was singing to himself. Many fathoms deep he rested in the cool, dark sea, his great voice echoing for miles through the ocean.

On and on he sang, at a whale's pace. It was a very long song, indeed, and he repeated it over and over again. Some of it he had learned from his mother and older whales and the rest was his own invention. He liked to sing alone almost as much as he liked to sing with his friends in a school chorus.

Somehow, Humpety didn't have to breathe in and out as he sang. If he had, he would most probably have drowned. Instead he was able to move the air around the inside of his enormous mouth and throat to make all kinds of sounds, like mewing seagulls, howling wolves, roaring thunder, jet planes screaming, motorbikes, sirens and giant canaries tweeting.

A tiny shrimp swam by and bumped against Humpety's eye.

"Oh, excuse me," stuttered Shrimp. "You're so big I didn't see you."

Humpety turned his eye and looked up at the tiny shrimp spinning in the water above him.

"Yes, I am big. In fact I am the biggest thing in the sea and probably the biggest animal in the world."

"I'm sure you are," replied Shrimp, wiping his long feelers and scratching his back clean. "Say, did you hear those terrible roars and rumbles? I thought there was a hole in the earth and the sea was gurgling down it."

Humpety didn't like Shrimp's description of his singing. He snorted, "It was me singing, and according to my cousins, the dolphins, I am very musical."

"Tell me," said the shrimp, "is it true that the dolphins can use their voices to find things in the dark like the sonar on those people's ships''

''Yes, and they give me a headach, too,'' said Humpety.

Shrimp thought for awhile and then said, ''Dolphins must be the most intelligent of all who live in the sea then.''

''But I'm the biggest and most important,'' the whale replied at once.

''Oh, no, we shrimps are the most important,'' said Shrimp, ''because there are more of us than you and we keep this place clean.''

Humpety blew a bubble and nearly lost his cool. ''Don't be ridiculous,'' he said. ''I'm a mammal, even if size doesn't count. I'm a mammal and you're just a shell thing with no bones.''

''Yes, a crustacean you mean,'' said Shrimp. ''Thanks for reminding me. Our kind were here long before the likes of you ever evolved, so that makes us even more important.''

Just then a dolphin swam by, and the whale and the shrimp called for him to settle their argument. Dolphin listened carefully to the reasons each thought he was the most important. He then pronounced: ''We each have our place and we all depend on each other. A shrimp is a shrimp and a whale is a whale. No one, on land or sea, is more important than anyone else.''

Humpety and Shrimp thanked the wise dolphin. Then Humpety said, ''Ouch, I have an itch in the middle of my back and I can't reach it. Please scratch it for me, Shrimp.''

Shrimp obliged willingly, finding a little cut on the whale's back that he happily ate clean. Humpety soon felt better, and he made up a song for the shrimp that went like this:

"Too big I was to see
You are just as important as me.
Although you are small, yes ever so wee,
You are just as important as me."

"As I," said the shrimp. "As me," said the whale. "No, 'as I' is correct grammar," sang Shrimp. So they swam together, with Shrimp and Humpety singing, "As I. As me. As we. As us." It was a very fine chorus!

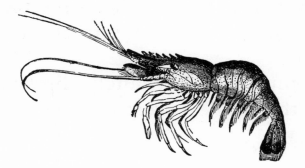

# THE ANT
# AND THE
# GRASSHOPPER

naware that a grasshopper was watching him, Ant was struggling to drag a crumb of bread six times his own size towards home. The ant and hundreds of other workers were clearing up the remains of a human's picnic. They would store some of the food in their underground city and give the rest to other ants who stayed in the city and labored to keep it clean and in good repair. They would also feed the city guards who had the job of keeping robber

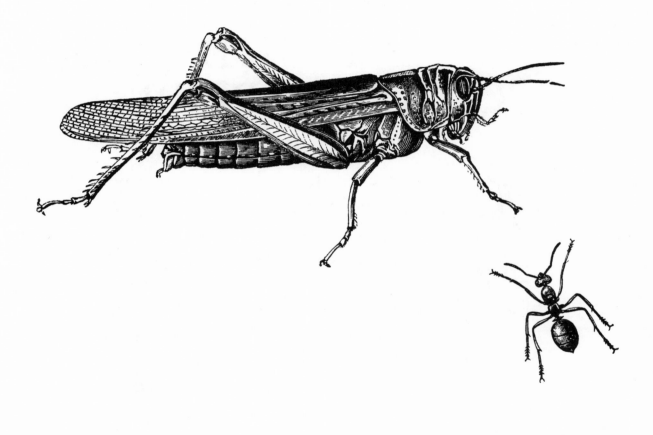

ants away and of warning the city of invasion by other ant colonies.

The grasshopper spoke to the little ant, who was so surprised that he let go of the bread and it rolled into a deep gully. "You are always so busy, you ants," said the grasshopper, who talked by rubbing his legs and wings together. "You and the bees are such hard workers. Do you ever enjoy life?"

"Look what you made me do," complained the ant, who was desperately trying to pull the bread out of the gully. Fortunately, another ant came to help, and they soon had the bread back on the trail. The trail, which led to and from the picnic area and their city, had been marked with scent by scout ants who had discovered the picnic earlier that afternoon. Their marks on the trail pointed the way for the food collectors, so no one would get lost. The world is a big place for an ant.

The second ant decided to drag the bread the rest of the way back to the city. The first ant sat up and wiped its antennae, his sense organs, before returning to collect more food.

"Getting ready for another load?" the grasshopper asked, further irritating the ant.

"Yes," replied the ant, "I can't talk now, there's work to be done. You other good-for-nothing insects, you're just a lazy bunch of layabouts. Work is what makes an ant an ant and that's what life's about."

The grasshopper twitched his antennae and jumped down from his perch onto a long blade of grass. Facing the little ant, he looked closely at him and said, "Look friend, I don't want to preach; but some say too much work isn't good for you. I like to sing in the sun and fly around and enjoy life.''

''That's your way, but I have responsibilities,'' replied the ant. ''I have much work to do for the city and a queen ant to attend who will lay next year's workers. Now please get off the trail, you're in our way.''

Just then three ants struggled by pushing and pulling a raisin. One ant, in a very important-sounding and official voice, said, ''Out of the way, Grasshopper! Back to work, Number X3142.''

''Now, who was that?'' the hopper asked as the work party passed by.

''That's our supervisor,'' Ant replied, ''And I must get back to the work shift now.''

''Goodbye, Ant,'' Grasshopper called as the hard-worker raced along the trail. ''Just like people,'' said the hopper to himself, ''They're always too busy to enjoy life, busy, busy, doin', doin', instead of just being and letting be.''

''But we have the biggest city and the best society in the world,'' another ant responded as it raced by to collect another load.

''You don't know what you're missing,'' chirruped the hopper, as he rose up happily in the air, snapping his wings to make a volley of loud clicks to tell other hoppers who and where he was.

Just then a blackbird swopped down and caught him in mid flight. ''See what happens to lazy, do-nothings,'' called one of the ants.

''It's my destiny,'' said the grasshopper. ''I'm no slave who lives only to work for a fat queen. I enjoy life and now someone is enjoying me!'' With that, he disappeared inside the bird's mouth forever.

''Some bugs just live a day at a time,'' X31442 said to his workmates, X5410 and X7222. ''I guess it's fun for some just to play all day long, but we have responsibilities.''

''That's right,'' said their supervisor. ''We have a society, and we all help each other. If we didn't cooperate to build a city and store food we couldn't live through the winter. Remember, a lone ant is a dead ant. Our strength and wisdom is in our togetherness.''

''Then we're superior to grasshoppers and other solitary bugs, aren't we?,'' said X3142.

''No,'' said the older supervisor. ''Nobody is superior, and we each have our place in nature. Now, back to work fellows, and tonight we will all feast in the warmth and security of our great city.''

# THE RAVEN
# AND
# THE COYOTE

ager with anticipation, Pancho was excited because this was the first time that he had been allow-ed to go with his parents on a hunt. Anytime before, when he or one of his three littermates tried to follow them, they would growl and send their cubs scurrying back to the den. But now they were old and strong enough to travel long distances, for a hunter must have stamina and be ready for anything.

67

## The Raven and the Coyote

The coyote family made their way over the dry scrubland, alert for the slightest movement or faintest scent on the breeze that might mean food. After an hour or so they had found nothing, and Pancho's feet were sore from sharp rocks and thorns. Hunting, it seemed, was not as easy as he had first thought. They rested for awhile in the shade of a tree, and Pancho was almost asleep when he noticed his parents looking intently into the sky. A large raven was flying fast and low, cawing excitedly. ''Just a big black bird,'' thought Pancho, as he scratched himself and rolled onto his side to sleep. Before he was able to close his eyes, he found himself suddenly on his feet and following his parents whose eyes never left the raven.

Soon they heard another raven calling from a tree above a dry creek, and the bird they were following was flying directly toward it. Pancho wondered if his parents had some incredible plan to catch the birds. A moment later, he understood. There in the creek lay the half-eaten remains of a deer, killed by a cougar. The coyote family feasted that day, thanks to the ravens who had found the kill first and whom his wise parents had followed.

A few months later, Pancho was almost full-grown, and he knew that it was time to leave his family and seek his fortune in some distant hunting range. There was not enough food in the area for a family of full-grown coyotes. So Pancho and his litter-mates departed, each going off in a different direction.

Pancho traveled for several days until he came to an area of scrubland in a high plateau between the mountains. It seemed like a good place to settle, and there were plenty of jack rabbits and other game for him to hunt. After a few months, though, food became harder and harder to find. One day he saw a raven flying and cawing loudly. He followed it, hoping to find a meal as he had once with his parents. But the raven was only flying to its mate, and Pancho went hungry. He looked up at the ravens and yipped, "I'm hungry and I've followed you for miles. Where's my dinner?"

The ravens ignored the rude young coyote and preened their feathers leisurely for awhile. Pancho grew impatient and jumped up against the tree and howled for attention.

"Young coyote," said one of the ravens, "You should know that ravens don't always fly toward food; but, like you, we travel from place to place for all kinds of reasons. This is our favorite lookout spot. If we are lucky and you are patient, we might find a meal today.''

Later that day the ravens did find food, most of which Pancho ate greedily.

Two days later Pancho sat down under the tree again and waited for the ravens. His empty stomach growled with hunger. He snapped at a fly that kept buzzing around his head and caught it. It was sweet, but its taste only made him more impatient for food.

''You really are a lazy fellow,'' cawed one of the ravens as he flew to the lookout tree. ''There are lots of grasshoppers around and they make good eating.''

"That's too much hard work. Anyway, there are never enough of them to satisfy my hunger," he whimpered.

"Have it your own way," replied the raven.

Pancho grew sleepy in the heat of the day and eventually dozed off. Suddenly he heard a caw and the ravens were flying away. He leaped up and raced behind them. In a short while they came upon the remains of a dead porcupine. "There's nothing left of it to eat," Pancho growled, "I should eat you instead." Angrily he leaped at the nearest raven and held it against the ground under his front paws.

"Eat me and it will be your last meal," the raven croaked. "Without me, you will never find another meal until this drought is over and the rains come." Pancho didn't listen. With a swift bite he killed the bird and ate it, feathers and all. ''That feels better,'' he said to himself, as he licked his lips. ''A bit tough and bony, but it was food anyway.'' He wondered where the other raven had gone and when it would lead him to more food. However, the other raven, a female, had flown far away and would never return after she had seen her mate killed.

Pancho was alone now and feeling hungry again. ''Perhaps I shouldn't have killed my friend after all,'' he thought, as he chewed on a worthless old piece of deerskin he had found. Several days later Pancho was too weak to move and he went to sleep for the last time. Soon after, two young ravens saw the remains of the dead coyote. They flew down and feasted on what was left of Pancho. ''Just a few more days until the rains," cawed one of them. "I wonder why this skinny fellow didn't follow our cousins, like other coyotes, and find food together. I feel badly for eating a friend. Perhaps he was a stupid coyote and let his hunger get the better of him."

Indeed, he was a stupid coyote and it was too late now for him to learn better. The old raven had been right. Pancho had eaten the one friend who might have saved him, and that last meal cost him his life.

# THE FOX,
# THE COYOTE
# AND THE WOLF

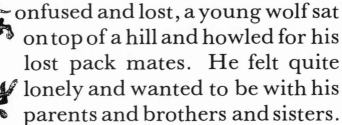onfused and lost, a young wolf sat on top of a hill and howled for his lost pack mates. He felt quite lonely and wanted to be with his parents and brothers and sisters. A young coyote heard the wolf cub's howls. He joined his cousin on the hill and began to yip and howl, too.

"I'm lonely, Coyote. Don't make fun of me," said the wolf cub.

## The Fox, The Coyote and The Wolf

"Well, I'm here," said the coyote. "Two's company and three's a crowd, that's what we coyotes say."

A red fox, whose den was nearby, heard the wolf and the coyote and skipped up the hill. She sat a few yards away from them.

"What's all this noise about?" she demanded, eyeing the two critically. "All you wolves ever do is run all over the place together. And you coyotes! Two of you make as much noise as a pack of ten wolves."

Coyote and Wolf looked at her in silence and she twitched her tail nervously.

"Well, you know what I mean," she said.

"I heard you say we coyotes are a noisy bunch and that the wolves are just a gang of good for nothings," replied Coyote.

"Yes," said the fox, "why can't you be quiet and civil like us foxes and mind your own business. Why do you have to make so much noise, Coyote?"

"I take it you prefer to live alone?" inquired the wolf.

"Yes," said Fox, "for most of the year we foxes like to live alone. Some of us never marry. We prefer the quiet life."

"And you expect everyone else to do as you do?" queried the coyote.

"Of course," said the fox.

"Do you know that if we wolves lived alone like you, we would starve to death?" said the wolf cub. "We hunt big animals like deer and it takes several of us to catch one. We couldn't all live on mice and insects like you."

"And," said Coyote, "if we lived like you, we would fight with you over the same things to eat. As it is, we coyotes fit in just nicely between the wolves and the foxes, and both of us eat the leftovers of the wolf packs' dinners, too."

"I see what you mean," said the fox after thinking it over for awhile. "I thought I was better than either of you and that you should follow my ways. I guess I was wrong. Please accept my apologies, dear cousins."

Just then a wolf howled in a deep voice from about a mile away, and the wolf cub said, "That's my dad. I'm off. See you again, friends."

The fox and the coyote understood now why the cub wanted to join up with the pack. He wasn't a softie, afraid of being alone. It was the way of the wolf to be with others of his own kind. His survival depended upon it.

"See you around, Fox," yipped the coyote as he set off to join his mate in the valley below.

The fox returned to her home to hunt for insects and mice. Unlike the wolf, she preferred to live alone, and unlike the coyote, she didn't care to have a steady mate all the time.

"I guess I'm happy being a fox," she said to herself as she poked around in the grass after an elusive field mouse, "And being a coyote or a wolf is neither better nor worse than being a fox. That's just the way things are."

# THE COYOTE AND THE PRAIRIE DOG

"Wow-wee!" howled Threepaws. "I haven't seen the likes of you around for ages! No, don't run down into your hole. I want to chat with you, not eat you."

Warily, the little prairie dog sat on the hard rim of his hole which led into an underground prairie dog 'city.' His nose and tail twitched nervously as he looked uncertainly at the old coyote who had hailed him. Threepaws had lost a paw in a trap put out

by a rancher a long time ago. He was surprised to find the prairie dog, since most of
their cities had been wiped out by ranchers,
who wanted to have all the land for their
sheep and cattle and would never share it
with wild animals.

The ranchers had been after Threepaws
for years because he sometimes killed sheep
when he was very hungry, even though he
didn't like their taste. What else could he do,
since there was little else to eat? And
anyway, what if he did take the occasional
sheep. It was his land as much as the ranchers. It was they who had replaced his
natural diet with their sheep.

With little else living in the prairie but
sheep, no one could blame the coyote for
eating them. But the greedy ranchers did,
and Threepaws was an outlaw. After being

shot at again and again, he decided to move to the hills at the edge of the praire. It was here that he had come across the prairie dog town.

"Last stand of the prairie dogs," he whistled to the little animal sitting up by its hole.

"That's right," chattered the prairie dog. "There are twelve of us in this town and soon there will be babies. I hope we will soon have a city as we did in the old days."

"Yes," whined Threepaws. "Seeing is believing. I thought you were all gone forever. I remember when there were dozens of cities around here. Life is hard these days. I wish you luck and I won't tell anyone you're here."

## The Coyote and the Prairie Dog

"Thank you, Coyote," squeaked the prairie dog, "Look out for traps, poison baits and things yourself!"

Just then they saw a rancher approaching on horseback and he was heading straight for the prairie dog town. Threepaws knew what to do at once. He ran flattened low to the ground so as not to be seen and then at a safe distance from the prairie dogs he stood up and barked at the horseman. If he had been a bird like a plover, or a deer, he might have dragged one of his limbs as though he were injured. In this way some animals can lure a hunter away from their nests or infants.

The horseman chased Threepaws for about a mile and then gave up when the coyote just seemed to vanish into thin air. In fact, Threepaws was lying down very close to the rancher, but because his coat color blended with the yellow and gray earth he was quite invisible!

That night Threepaws felt so happy that he howled and yipped to the moon. Now the prairie dogs knew that they had at least one friend in the world. But unfortunately, Threepaw's howling broke the secret. Two men camping in the hills nearby heard him and decided to search the area thoroughly for signs of wildlife. The next day, they found the prairie dog town.

But, unlike the ranchers, these were men who studied and understood animals and wanted to protect them. One camped near the prairie dog town to guard it and the other went off for several days. When he returned, he came with metal stakes and several signs which he put in a great circle around the prairie dog city. Soon after, a dirt road was graded and then people started to come, driving by slowly to look at the prairie dogs. Threepaws was puzzled. Although so many people came by, none of the prairie dogs were ever killed. In fact, their city was beginning to grow. If he could have read the posted signs, he would have understood. They declared, **Prairie Dog City. National Refuge. No Trespassing.**

Thanks to Threepaws, the prairie dogs would live without disturbance from man.

# THE WOLF
# AND
# THE TRAPPER

 trapper was camping out in the forest, tired after a hard day of setting traps to catch whatever he could. He hoped to trap beaver by the river, and fox, bobcat and racoon in the woods. Their fur was valuable and he could sell their pelts for a lot of money.

Although he knew that the animals suffered when they were caught in the steel-jawed traps that he put out for them, he was not deliberately cruel. He felt it was right to ''harvest'' them in this way so he could earn a living. He never really asked himself if this were right or if he could make a good living some other way.

He was glad that people liked to wear the fur and skins of wild animals because that made him prosper. As he put a pot of coffee to brew on his campfire, he nearly spilled it when a wolf began to howl from a nearby hill. Soon another wolf answered, and then another, and another. He counted four in all, and they were howling in a circle around him.

The trapper grabbed his gun for protection and put more wood on the fire to make a bright blaze to keep the wolves away. Although he had been trapping and hunting for many years, he still didn't really understand any of the animals that he killed. He thought the wolves might attack him. He didn't know that wild wolves are too afraid to ever attack people.

But the poor man was afraid also, so he kept the fire blazing all night and never slept a wink. If he had known that the wolves were just curious and were howling to each other as a signal to come together to sleep for the night, he might have slept himself.

At dawn, stiff and tired, he ate a good breakfast and then set off to inspect his traps and to track the wolves. He had hopes of shooting one of them.

In his traps he found a red fox, two racoons and and old opossum. He hit each animal over the head to kill it, since a bullet would damage the pelt and lower its value. He threw the dead 'possum away because its ratty fur was of no value to him. It had died for nothing.

Then at the end of the trap line in the very last trap, he found a wolf. It had been chasing a deer with the rest of the pack and accidentally stepped into the trap. The man was delighted to see that the big wolf had a fine coat. He raised his club to strike the wolf. But before the club fell, the wolf said, "I kill to live, but you and your kind live to kill."

The trapper replied, "Some say you wolves should be left alone because you kill old and sick deer and fawns, if there are too many. You keep the deer herds in good shape. I say that might be, but you are all mean bloody killers and deserve to die."

"But hunting is our way, bloody as it may seem to you. We wolves obey the laws of nature, but what of you, man? You also kill, so why should we be persecuted?''

''I make my own laws and the world is man's to command,'' shouted the trapper.

''You kill for money, for the value of my fur,'' growled the wolf, ''and in killing wolves and other animals you upset the balance of nature. You are guilty of breaking the law.''

''I don't go by the laws of nature. I make the laws,'' the trapper hissed as he swung the club to smash the wolf's skull.

The trapper did not know that he had killed the last female wolf in the area. The other wolves were all males. There would be no more cubs and soon no more wolves left in the wild. If the trapper had known this, perhaps he would have cared, if only because there would be no more wolves to trap and shoot.

In some distant city, a man now wears a coat made of wolf fur. It cost a lot of money and he is proud to wear it, but if he really knew how the she wolf was killed he would hide his coat in shame and mourn the deaths of wolves. For if people continue to trap and kill them soon there will be none. Even if they and other wild creatures were protected, so that there would be plenty for the trapper, is it right to kill just for profit and pleasure?

# THE EAGLE
# AND
# THE CONDOR

eeping himself amused, the young bald eagle was enjoying his flying games in the hot air currents above a deep valley. Since the air rises in these currents or therms, he could fly effortlessly in a spiral, like a glider. Then from a great height, sometimes almost a mile, he would utter his piercing scream of a war cry, and suddenly swoop all the way down like a bolt of lightning. He felt very strong and

powerful on this day because no other bald eagle occupied the valley. Today it was his alone.

Quite unknown to young Baldy, an old condor, the largest flying bird in the world, was watching his aerobatics from his perch on a nearby cliff. Then, as Baldy began to climb up slowly on an air current, the condor silently glided towards him.

"Good day, young eagle, my name is Altar. What is yours?"

Baldy nearly closed his wings and fell to the ground in surprise. Collecting his composure he replied, "My name is Baldy. Of course you must know we are the most famous of birds. The people who live below, in what they call America, regard me as their national emblem."

"Yes," said the Condor, "a bird who hunts and kills is an appropriate choice for such people."

"Why do you say that?" said Baldy, taken aback.

"Well," said Altar, "just look around you. Where are all the mountain lions, the wolves, the bobcats and even the deer? Look at their sickly cattle and sheep. Hungry coyotes often eat them, so the ranchers put out poisoned meat. If any of us or the coyotes eat that meat, we will die. Some of us even get caught in steel-jaw traps intended to catch the coyotes. And look at their fields of corn and other crops, all sprayed with poisonous chemicals to kill the insects. Do you know what happens then?"

"No," said Baldy, circling higher and higher just above the great condor.

## Lessons From Nature

"You mean to tell me your parents never told you?" squawked Altar in surprise.

"No," replied Baldy, "I had no parents, at least not real parents. People raised me. My parents were shot, along with several other eagles, by men from planes. Some man who had been watching our nest for days took me and my sister and raised us himself. I hatched from my shell, but my sister never hatched from hers. He released me here later, in this valley where I had been born."

"Ah-ha," said Altar. "I thought you looked familiar. You do resemble your father. Do you know why your parents died young man, and why your sister never hatched?"

"No," said Baldy. "I guess I have a lot to learn. The man friend only taught me how to hunt for small birds and rabbits and things."

"Your parents and other eagles died because several farmers hired a hunter to shoot you out of the skies. They blamed you for the death of their lambs."

The condor continued, "They also trapped and poisoned the coyotes for the same reason. Since you eagles and coyotes eat rabbits and mice, the same animals which eat the ranchers' sheep grass, you'd think they'd have appreciated you. Admittedly, some very hungry eagles and coyotes took an occasional lamb when other food was scarce, but this was nothing compared to what they saved by keeping the rabbits and mice down."

"What about that poison chemical stuff?" asked Baldy.

"Hmm," said Altar and the air hissed through his great wings as he checked his speed. "Chemicals are terrible. DDT is sprayed on the plants to kill insects, and many of the birds and mice that we eat are full of DDT because they ate some of the poisoned grain and insects."

"Then what happens?" asked Baldy.

"Our chicks die before, or soon after they hatch, or the egg shells are so thin they break soon after they are laid."

"And what of you, Altar?" inquired Baldy.

"I am the last of my kind on earth," sighed Altar.

"What can we do?" asked Baldy.

"Follow me, my friend," said Altar. "Do not be afraid." The two birds rose together until they were mere specks in the sky. And then they seemed to disappear. There was no place left on earth for them, and there would be no more like them ever again. They had become extinct.

# THE CAT
# AND
# THE DOG

ith self-importance Felina curled up on the window ledge to bask in the sun. She was an aristocratic Persian cat who shared the same home with Spot. Their owners loved both of them very much and Spot and Felina were the best of friends. When it was cold, or when she just wanted to feel close, Felina would snuggle up to Spot, who was a big, shaggy, easy-going mongrel dog. He liked to chase other cats outside although he never

intended to catch or harm them: that was just good sport. Indoors, though, he was a very quiet and well-mannered fellow — most of the time, that is. Sometimes Felina would lick his face and he enjoyed that very much, but when he tried to lick hers in thanks, she always avoided his kisses. One lick with his big wet tongue would muss her fur. She was a fussy cat and very careful about her looks.

"You are such a loyal and obedient servant, Spot," purred Felina.

"Mmmm," Spot whined in reply. "A good dog is an obedient dog, that's what they say."

"Yes," replied Felina, "that's what you were taught when you were a puppy. It really amazes me how you always do as they say. They say "come" and you come, "sit" and you sit, "down" and you get down, "walk time" and you get your leash, and . . ."

Spot didn't let her continue. He was embarrassed by her teasing. "I obey them to show that I love them," he replied.

Felina sighed, "I don't have to obey them, Spot, although I still love them. But you are a dog and that's expected of you."

"Yes, I know," said Spot. "They always boss me around because I'm a dog. I wish I could always have my own way like you, Felina. You can do anything you like. If I'm disobedient, and get punished I feel as if no one loves me.

They heard their owners coming and grew silent. Felina cooly blinked at them and stood up and yawned, sticking her tail in the air ready to be petted. Spot wagged his tail wildly and jumped up, trying to kiss his mistress on the face.

"Get down, Spot," she said. "You nearly knocked the lampstand over. Why can't you have good manners like Felina, you big clumsy, loveable oaf!"

Spot whined and crawled under the table, feeling guilty. "See, no one loves me," he said to himself. He was too good-natured to feel jealous about Felina who was now being stroked and cuddled.

Suddenly, Felina jumped off the windowsill and onto the velvet armchair. She rolled over, purring, waiting for more attention.

"Oh, you smart aleck," said her mistress. "You know you're not supposed to be on that chair. It shows every hair, you little witch." And, with that, her master and mistress both tickled her tummy and fussed over her.

Felina jumped down after she had had enough and meowed to Spot, who was still under the table. "You see, a cat can get away with anything."

Spot bounded out and leaped into the arm chair, and with tail wagging and mouth open in a big grin, rolled over to be tickled just like Felina.

"Get down, you bad, bad dog!" both his owners shouted at once. "How dare you!" He felt his master's heavy hand slap his behind.

"I lost again," he thought as he once more hid under the table. "Felina always gets to do what I can never do," he thought with jealousy. This made him feel angry, but much worse was the feeling that no one loved or understood him.

## The Cat and The Dog

"What gets into that dog, I don't know," his master muttered as he walked into the kitchen. "He sure tries to be a cat sometimes!"

"I'm no cat," Spot growled to himself.

"No, you're certainly not," purred Felina, "but you will always be unhappy if you try to be something that you're not. Remember that you're a dog and you must always do what is expected of you," she said kindly. "Just try being yourself and they will surely love you."

Hesitantly, Spot followed his master into the kitchen, and sat by the doorway quietly. He gave a gentle "woof" and wagged his tail, a faint grin appearing as he pulled his lips back in his most friendly and polite expression.

"Come to apologize, or is it food you

want?'' said his master, tauntingly. But Spot just sat there. Then his mistress came to the doorway and said, ''Jim, don't tease Spot, he has come to apologize.''

''No, Debbie,'' he replied, ''I just can't stand dogs who get jealous or too excited and then knock things over and are disobedient.''

''But Jim, Spot feels unloved when we discipline him and seem to favor Felina. What can we do to let him know we love him?''

''Woof,'' said Spot, and he grabbed at his leash hanging on the kitchen door.

''Take him for a walk, with fun and games in the park,'' Jim retorted with a laugh as he clipped the leash onto Spot's collar. From then on, Jim and Debbie knew how to show their love, and Spot, at last, felt wanted and understood.

# ANIMALS
# OF
# FOREIGN LANDS

# THE PEACOCK
# WHO HAD
# A PROBLEM

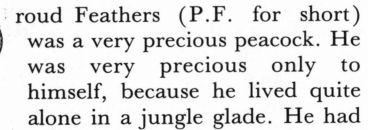

roud Feathers (P.F. for short) was a very precious peacock. He was very precious only to himself, because he lived quite alone in a jungle glade. He had all he needed here: fresh water from a spring, and fruit and seeds from the trees and bushes. He stayed inside his small clearing because if he went into the thick jungle beyond, he would surely damage his fine tail feathers against thorn bushes and fallen branches. Anyway, it was dangerous out there and P.F. knew that if he had to fly to avoid danger, such as a hungry leopard, his beautiful feathers would soon be in tatters.

When P.F. was very young, before he even knew that he was to become a peacock, he met his father one day by the river. His mother, a plain-looking peahen, clucked and fussed over her chicks as their father came near. Then he bowed in front of her and fanned out his magnificent tail. Each 'eye' flashed and winked as he slowly turned and waved his tail feathers in the sunlight. P.F. was most impressed and from then on he decided that he was going to be the most handsome peacock in the jungle, with the longest and flashiest tail of all.

When he was a little older he noticed some new feathers growing that had eye spots on them. How proud he was to be growing up at last. He paraded in front of his brothers and sisters. Hardly had he begun to show off when the alarm call of a jungle fowl made them all fly for cover into the dense vegetation of the jungle.

When P.F. looked at his tail again he found that three of the four new feathers had been torn to shreds by the bushes. After a few days though, more began to grow but, to his great concern, he again ruined them in the bushes flying away from danger.

How could he ever grow a fine tail like his father's? P.F. thought about this for a long while and then he found the solution. He would find a quiet place in the jungle where he could let his tail grow in peace.

After a couple of years his tail was indeed fantastic, and P.F. would parade and bow down by the stream where his reflection was mirrored in the still pools of water.

"I'm surely the most magnificent peacock in the world," he said to himself. Then he let out a piercing "Meeoww" scream. That was the call that all peacocks make when they feel important. No peacocks ever answered and after a few more months P.F. began to feel lonely. He was getting a little bored admiring himself in the water and it would be more fun showing off to other peacocks and impressing the lady hens with his dazzling eyes.

"If I go back to them I will have to get through that jungle somehow. It will certainly ruin my feathers. Then no one would look at me. My tail is so big now I might not even be able to fly away from danger. I might even get stuck in the bushes and get eaten alive.''

But the longer he stayed in the glade, the more he yearned to be with his friends. So one morning he began the long journey back home through the jungle. At first, the going was easy along a trail made by the deer. Many times, though, he had to rush into hiding when he heard something big coming along the trail. Whenever a squirrel, monkey or jungle fowl gave an alarm call, P.F. would leap into the air and fly into hiding until the jungle was quiet and safe again.

His tail was much shorter than when he set out, and the beautiful feathers were now broken, shredded, and dull. ''I can't go home like this. Everyone will laugh at me,'' he clucked unhappily to himself. ''Nor can I go back. I'm nearly home and I'm never going back along that scary trail again, tail or no tail.''

A short time later he arrived at the familiar home by the river where he was born. He saw some peacocks and hens under the old banyan tree and he stopped in his tracks when they saw him. No one recognized him, and one of the cocks puffed out his chest and started to put his tail up to frighten poor P.F. ''Wait,'' said one of the hens, running forward. ''Look, it's Proud Feathers! The others looked more closely and they knew it was P.F. when they called his name and he bowed his head. P.F. felt ashamed and kept his head down, ready to be teased and tormented. ''Look at his tail'' said one of them, ''it's such a mess!'' and another said, ''He must have faced many dangers to get into such a state. What a brave fellow he must be.''

Soon P.F. was surrounded by his friends and was welcomed home like a hero. Later he told them the truth and they all laughed together. ''I'm happier now that I ever was, alone in the glade. Who needs to be all fancy and feathered up to impress others. You like me even without a fine tail and I had thought you wouldn't even look at me if I wasn't perfect.''

''Meeoww,'' he called, and all around him, his friends answered ''Meeoww'' ''Meeoww.''

P.F. knew that he would never be perfect and he didn't have to be anyway. His tail would soon repair itself, but that wasn't so important anymore.

# THE POUCHERS
# AND
# THE PLATYPUS

"Yes, my dear, it really is wonderful to be so special," said a kangaroo to her wallaby cousin as they sat back on their big tails to chat by the water hole.

"I know what you mean Roo," said Wally. "I mean I know, you know, what you mean."

"Of course dear Wally, isn't it wonderful to have tails like springs for leaping."

"And pouches for babies," added Wally.

## The Pouchers and the Platypus

"We stand up like people and our front legs are hands," observed Roo. She went on "I think, no, I know, dear Wally, you know, I know we are the most intelligent beasts in all this land."

"I know what you mean Roo," said Wally. "It's great to be great. You know what I mean."

Suddenly a platypus came out of her hole in the bank of the stream. She swam across the pool toward the two pouchers and said, "I heard you two chattering and making believe you're the best of all beasts in Australia. But look at me. I lay eggs like a crocodile. I have a bill like a duck, fur like a wallaby, a tail like a beaver, claws like a cat and feet like an otter. I say I'm the greatest of the greats and the best of the best."

"You are the strangest of the strange," said Roo.

"And the rarest of the rare, I mean, you know, the rarest of rarest you know; that I know," added Wally.

Platty was happy to be recognized and snapping her bill she swam back to the eggs in her den.

"Well did you ever?" asked Roo.

"No, I never," said Wally. "I never before saw anyone like that in my whole life. I'm afraid we're not so special at all. I mean after all. You know what I mean."

"I know," sighed Roo, as they hopped away, "but at least you know, it's nice to think that you're special."

"Unique," shouted Platty from her hole in the bank. "Just one of a kind, and so are you! Be happy my friends, hop high, we're all the greatest, the best, the rarest and strangest of all.''

''She's right, you know,'' said Roo.

''I know,'' said Wally and they hopped along together singing: ''I know, you know. You know, I know, you know.''

''I hope they really know,'' sighed Platty to herself, as she turned to check her eggs. ''I hope they know that everyone on earth is very special and everyone is quite unique. Being so, then everyone must respect each other, no matter how different or strange they look.''

# THE BACTRIAN CAMEL AND THE DROMEDARY

Looking more like a moth-eaten carpet than the champion racer of the desert that he once was, the old dromedary dozed under a palm tree. He was glad of the shade: it was 120° in the sun, and the Sahara desert that surrounded him for hundreds of miles was one of the hottest and dryest parts of the world. He had taken his master to this oasis, an isolated spot in the desert where water could be found and palm trees grew. Both Fez, the Arabian camel, and his

master, Abdul, had drunk their fill of the delicious, cooling water.

Without Fez, Abdul would have died from thirst. It was such a long journey across the desert that no man could do it without his camel. Horses can't stand the heat and a car's radiator would soon boil over. Also—there's nowhere to buy gasoline in the desert! A dromedary can go for days without water becasue the big 'hump' of fat on his back provides him with water in times of emergency. Fez had big feet too, that stopped him from sinking into the sand so he could stride easily and not get too tired. In his youth he was a great racer and had even beaten some of Abdul's friends' best Arabian horses. Fez had a special advantage on soft sand where his larger feet helped him move more quickly than the horses with their smaller hooves.

But now Fez was old and tired and his master wondered if they could make it to the next oasis. From there, it was only three days journey to their home. It was sunset and Abdul decided to begin the journey since it would be cooler travelling at night. A jackal howled and yipped as the first stars came out. Then over a dune came another traveller on his camel, a strong, young Bactrian camel that had not one, but two humps!

The two men talked for a while and after the newcomer and his camel had drunk and rested, they all set off together across the sand. The two camels glided along easily, like ships of the desert.

"You move like an old man," said Two-humps to Fez. "I bet you won't make it."

"If I take it easy and save my strength, I will," said Fez. "Why do you speak so unkindly?"

"Well," replied Two-humps, "I heard you were a great racer but I know I can beat you anytime."

"I'm sure you could," said Fez. "I'm retired from racing now." They walked along in silence for a while, but Two-humps still wanted to prove he was better than Fez.

"So you won't race me. I guess you're scared, seeing my strength and you with only one hump. I have two so that means I'm twice as good as you!"

"Save your strength and don't talk so much," sighed Fez.

## Lessons From Nature

All night Two-humps kept teasing him and racing ahead to show off his speed until his master would rein him back to a steady pace again.

By noon the next day it was roasting and there was no shady place to rest. The men walked along side of their camels for a while to give them a rest. Suddenly it grew dark and the sky was filled with flying sand. A sand storm! Rather than get lost, which would be easy under such conditions, the riders stopped. The men laid down against their camels who sheltered them from the stinging hot sand that the wind whipped into their eyes and noses.

"Scared Two-humps?" inquired Fez.

"Of c-course n-not," stuttered Two-humps who had never been in a sand storm like this before. He could hardly breathe and was sure that he was going blind.

"Relax and save your strength," Fez advised.

It was night before the storm passed over. Stiffly, old Fez got up but he felt rested and stronger. They travelled all through the night—but the next morning brought a bad omen. The water hole that was to give them water for the final 3 days' journey was dry! They had to continue without water. The riders had enough saved to see them through and Fez knew he could last it out. He could almost smell his home even at that great distance and his spirits lifted. He turned to Two-humps, but Two-humps was lying down by the dry water hole and refused to budge, in spite of his master's shouts and prods.

## Lessons From Nature

Two-humps was ready to give up. He had exhausted himself showing off and he felt afraid and hopeless now. He looked at Fez and said, "Goodbye, friend. I am going to die. I guess having two humps doesn't make me better than you."

"Your camel will feel more confident if we tie him onto my camel and pull him up," shouted Fez's master. Old as he was, Fez pulled with all his might and, once on his feet again, Two-humps did feel better.

"Follow me," said Fez, "and I will take you home safely." Two-humps was grateful and he promised never to tease camels that only had one hump ever again.

# THE PANDA
# AND
# THE PIG

ear the great mountains of China, where no people have ever lived, lies a deep valley. In this green and peaceful valley lived a panda bear and a wild pig. Both decided to settle there when they were quite young because there was so much food and it was such a beautiful place.

One evening, as the sun was slipping slowly behind the mountains and turning the skies red and gold, the panda bear and the pig met each other in a clearing in their valley.

They had heard each other snuffling and rooting around before, but this was the first time they met face to face.

"Hello!" snorted the pig. "My name is 'Rooter' because I'm always rooting in the earth with my tusks to find things to eat. You must be the quiet one I hear sometimes in the bamboo."

"Quite right," said Panda, sitting up and looking very neat and formal in his black and white suit. "You must be that noisy fellow that roots and squeals and snorts and eats all kinds of unmentionable things off the ground."

Rooter grunted and asked "Is bamboo the only thing you eat?"

"Quite so," replied Panda. "My parents only gave me what I wanted when I was young and that was bamboo. I eat nothing but the best. Only the sweetest and most tender bamboo shoots will do. That's how I keep in shape.''

The pig looked at the round, ball-body of the panda and realized that for a panda, to be in shape must be to be as round as possible.

''Well, I eat anything I can find and there's plenty here in this valley, praise be,'' said the pig. ''In the valley where I was born there was little of anything to eat, so I moved here and am doing very well, thank you.''

The panda looked down his nose and said, ''Well, it was less disagreeable to meet you than I would have thought by the noise you make when you're eating.'' Then he rolled over and ambled away, not even turning to snuffle ''Goodbye'' when Rooter said politely ''Good to meet you, and thank you.''

## The Panda and The Pig

A few weeks later the air was filled with birds of many shapes and colors. The birds came in flocks from far and wide to feast on the bamboo. All the bamboo in the valley had blossomed, as it does about every 40 years, and the birds feasted on this 'rice' from the bamboo. After the bamboo blossoms, it dies and takes many years before it grows back again.

A month after the birds had cleaned up every grain of bamboo rice, the pig and the panda met again.

"Oh, dear me!" exclaimed the pig, "you *have* lost shape," and he stared at Panda whose empty skin hung like a loose sack around his thin body. "Whatever happened to you?"

"The bamboo flowered and died and I have nothing to eat," moaned the panda. "I was too fat and lazy to move out and find another valley when it started to bloom and now I'm almost too weak to move.''

"But there's plenty of food," Rooter squealed. "Just look around under you—use your paws and dig," exlcaimed Rooter.

The panda tried, but whatever he found he refused to eat. "It's no use," he sighed, "I was born and raised on the best; bamboo shoots are all I can eat."

"This is ridiculous," snorted the pig. But it was soon too late. The next morning the panda was dead.

"How sad and stupid," sighed Rooter as he snuffled away a tear and began to dig around for his breakfast. "Thank heavens that I never insisted on having only what I thought was the best. And how lucky I was that my parents never gave in to me and let me eat just what I wanted!"

# THE ZEBRA
# AND
# THE GIRAFFE

tripes, a young zebra, stood drinking at the water hole with other members of his herd and his friends the gazelles and gnus. It was a hot, dry day and many animals of the African plains of the Serengeti had migrated to other places in search of water.

While the animals were drinking, a tall and graceful giraffe came to the water hole to quench his thirst. It was difficult to reach the water which was in a deep hole surrounded by steep banks on all sides. His knees bent and he lowered his long neck by degrees until he was at last able to drink.

"Look at that ridiculous fellow," whinnied the zebra. "Hey, long neck," he shouted. "I bet it's cold up there when you stand up. Do you ever get dizzy—and what do you do if you get a stiff neck?"

Slowly the giraffe stood up and cooly looking down at the others replied, "I am the tallest animal in the world and I feel fine. If I look ridiculous to you, I might add that your black and white stripes look a little jazzy to me."

"They camouflage me in the tall grass against lions and hunting dogs," retorted the zebra. "I might look jazzy to you, but to me you look stupid."

## Lessons From Nature

The giraffe chose to ignore the rude fellow and went his way. Later that day he met a hungry young lion who chased him for a short distance. Then Longneck turned and said, "Look, pussycat, I can outrun you any time, and if you try to attack me, I will hurt you with my powerful front feet. Some people around here think I'm stupid, but let me assure you . . . ." Before he could finish, the lion roared in disbelief and leaped at him. With one blow, he knocked the lion out cold with a karate-like flip of a long front leg. As the lion came to, still in disbelief, Longneck said, "Next time, pussycat, I'll split your head in two." Then he ambled off, searching for a tree with tender leaves that not even an elephant could reach.

A couple of weeks later Longneck met the same zebra, Stripes, who had been unkind to him earlier at the water hole.

## The Zebra and The Giraffe

"Well, Stripes, you don't look so good to me," said the giraffe.

"No," replied Stripes, "I'm starving. There's no grass left and with the drought there'll be none for a long time. I know I'll be in a lion's stomach soon."

Longneck continued to browse on a few leaves high up in a tree that no one else could reach. A few fell onto Stripes, who ate them up greedily.

"I see that a long neck can be useful," Stripes observed with great admiration. Longneck looked down at him and blinked.

"Yes," he replied, after thinking for awhile. "There aren't many of us and there's always plenty to go around for those who eat in the tree tops. Stick around Stripes and you can eat what I drop."

Stripes did, and he survived the drought.

He never teased a giraffe again, nor any other animal for that matter. No matter how funny they looked—with horny sides like the rhinoceros, mangy manes like the lions, furry faces like the gnus, and comical behinds like the baboons, Stripes never made fun of them again. He knew that everything had its purpose and place, and that even though a giraffe might look ridiculous, it had a very sensible neck — one that had saved his own neck!

# THE MONGOOSE
# AND
# THE COBRA

n the jungle there is an ancient Indian temple which no one has used for hundreds of years. It was built by a local king of the Nilgiri Valley and his people used it to worship the great spirits that looked over their cattle and crops. The descendants of these people now have a new temple and no one ever goes near the old temple because they fear the snakes that live in the cool darkness of the crumbling ruins.

## The Mongoose and the Cobra

The stone steps in front of the old temple were being slowly lifted up by the roots of a banyan tree which grew right through the roof of the temple. Under these steps lived a young cobra. He would glide silently out of his home early in the morning and hunt for his breakfast. Then he would lie on the stone steps and bask in the sun, his long body bulging where his breakfast was being digested. When the sun became too hot, he retired to his cool home.

One morning he met another young cobra who had moved into the area and was looking for a place to live. He didn't like this intruder who ignored his scent that, like a flag, marked the area where he lived as being his territory. Angrily, he hissed and extended his hood, a wide flap of skin around his head that made him look more terrifying than ever. The stranger was unafraid and rose up, hissing, to challenge the resident.

The two snakes wrestled together for a long time, each trying to push the other over and hold it to the ground. However, neither tried to bite the other to inject their poisonous venom. Cobras, like human wrestlers, follow certain rules, and the cobras' built-in rule is to never use their venom on each other.

Suddenly, after a tremendous struggle, the exhausted stranger gave up. The resident cobra let him slither away and he returned to the steps to bask in the sun.

He felt very satisfied with his victory and after a short rest, set out to hunt for breakfast.

## The Mongoose and The Cobra

Out later than usual, he met an un-expected neighbor for the first time: an old mongoose.

People in the village would sometimes tame a baby mongoose and keep it because when it grew up it would kill or drive off any cobras that came near the houses. A cobra is incredibly fast when it strikes but a mongoose is even faster. Somehow it outwits the snake, dodging its strike and in one instant, by twisting around, it kills the cobra with a single bite through the back of the neck.

When the old mongoose met the young cobra, he stood up slowly and said, "Good day neighbor. I can see that you are hunting late today. I hope I am not in your way." The old mongoose did not enjoy killing; he preferred to live in peace and avoid fighting.

But the young cobra wanted to prove himself. He felt very important after his victory over the other cobra. Rising up and extending his hood he hissed, "You old slow and toothworn coward, I'll show you to fear my power and respect me."

"But I do respect you because I have no wish to kill you," the mongoose replied quietly. The cobra stiffened and the mongoose knew he was ready to strike.

Before he could say "Stop, there is no need to kill or to die," the cobra leaped at him like a steel spring. The fangs of the snake hit the dry earth as the mongoose twisted and bit the cobra through the neck. "I am sorry," said the mongoose, as the snake writhed and slowly died. "I could do nothing else and you will never live to learn your lesson."

## The Mongoose and The Cobra

The other cobra who had lost the wrestling contest earlier had been lying in the bushes nearby and had seen all. Cautiously he approached the mongoose and said, ''I wish to live in the temple, and I have learned your lesson well.''

The old mongoose welcomed his new neighbor and they lived peacefully together for many years. No cobra before had ever believed that a mongoose could kill it because none had ever lived to find out. This cobra was indeed a lucky one for he was the only cobra to know the faster speed of a mongoose. For this cobra, seeing was believing.

# THE MONKEY
# AND
# THE ELEPHANT

ama was a young macaque monkey who lived in the Indian jungle. He lived in a troop, which consisted not only of his parents and two elder sisters, but several cousins, aunts, uncles and even grandparents and great aunts and uncles. In all there were nearly forty of them. Because they have a funny tuft of hair on their heads, people call them 'Bonnet' macaques.

Rama always woke up at sunrise, just as the peacocks and other birds began to sing.

He and his troop would move through the treetops and find a fresh tree to feed on for breakfast. After awhile, one of the older leaders would give the signal and they would head for the river to drink. Other grown-ups served as guards on the lookout for panthers or wild dogs who might try to catch and eat them. In the trees they were safe, but on the ground it was a different matter. One hoot of alarm would send them all scurrying up the nearest tree.

The younger monkeys liked to play in the river, jumping over the stones, playing tag, leapfrog and "king of the rock," where one had to stop others from pushing it into the water. Although Rama was the smallest and youngest, he was quick and agile and would jump onto another rock instead of getting wet.

## Lessons From Nature

When the grown-ups had given the youngsters time enough to play, they would return to the treetops and rest, nap, or groom each other. Grooming was a favorite pastime, and one monkey would invite another to groom its fur from head to toe. Sometimes, three of four would huddle together and groom each other at the same time. No, they were not picking fleas or lice, but were enjoying a special ritual. Monkeys enjoy being touched and touching each other, like some people who like to have a gentle back rub or have their hair brushed.

One day, Rama heard crashing and exploding noises from a tall clump of bamboo and he scampered through the trees to watch an elephant at work. This one, a big tusker called Trumpety (who was always trumpeting to let others know he was king of the jungle), was eating his dinner. He used his powerful trunk to twist and break the thick bamboo, which made loud noises like firecrackers as it broke under his might. Rama was amazed at Trumpety's strength. After awhile, the elephant felt he was being watched and said, "What is your name, you who watches me?"

"My name is Rama and I wish I could be as strong and big as you, great Trumpety."

"Oh," replied the elephant. "So you are not satisfied with being what you are."

"Yes," said Rama. "If I was like you, I would be king of the jungle and no one would hunt me."

Just then the elephant scraped a front foot on the ground. Then he bellowed in pain. A long sharp bamboo thorn was stuck deep in his foot and he couldn't get it out. He told

Rama that he often got thorns in his feet and that was the price he paid for being so heavy and choosing to eat thorny bamboo.

"I can't get the thorn out with my trunk. I wish I had fingers like you," sighed Trumpety.

"I can help if you keep still," said Rama, and he climbed down and pulled the thorn out of the tusker's foot.

"Thank you, little one, you are a good and clever friend."

Rama scampered home to tell his friends about his adventure. he was happy that he could help such a great elephant, and proud too. He decided that he was quite happy to be a monkey even if he was small and not very strong. After all, elephants don't have hands.